COMMUNICATIONS CRASH COURSE:

Eleven Strategic Conversation
Frameworks for Everyday
Scenarios to Enhance Your Con-
versations and Confidence

Alixander Laffredo-Dietrich

COPYRIGHT AND DISCLAIMER

◆ ◆ ◆

Communications Crash Course: Eleven Strategic Conversation Frameworks for Everyday Scenarios to Enhance Your Conversations and Confidence by Alixander Laffredo–Dietrich
www.galhad.com

and the reader alone is responsible for his or her actions.

THANK YOU

◆ ◆ ◆

A lot of thanks go out to more people than I can list in a book; therefore, to those not listed but who have played a part in my success, I extend my sincerest thanks.

First, to Mom and Eric *– Your constant support of me, even in my worst days, will not get the justice it deserves by thanking you here. When I say I could not be anywhere close to where I am without you, I mean it.*

To Dad and Stacy *– The work ethic and strict sense of perseverance could have only been inherited from the environment you raised me in. You both taught me to make demands of myself to get what I want, even if it makes me uncomfortable, and that is a skill I would never trade away.*

To Uncle Barney *– Even in my darkest days I know there is somebody in this world who will always love me, thanks to you. Your gratitude for everything in life—the good, the bad, and the ugly—is something I admire in you.*

To my best friend, Tyler – *Your candidness has helped me stay true to my mission and your motivation has lifted me up when I feel like giving up. You are the hardest-working man I have ever met or will ever meet, and that among many other reasons is why I look up to you. I am proud to call you my best friend of fifteen years. Here's to fifteen more!*

To Spauldo – *There are many things I appreciate about you, but one in particular is your willingness and effort to keep people in your life. You deserve the best, my friend, and without your input, I would never have been inspired to write this book.*

To JB – *You are the person in my life who made my personal growth so successful. You were relentless in what you demanded from me so that I would grow, and you never let me get lazy. I can never thank you enough.*

To Jorge – *Thank you for teaching me to let go. If it were not for you, I would never have discovered what creativity means for me. And of course, thanks for starting the LC with me—I could not have done it without you.*

To my friends in 5217 – *For constantly pushing me forward while keeping my life entertaining—you are the best.*

To Somiah, Aaron, and Dr. Blackwell – *Thanks for your invaluable lessons and helping me discover my passion for entrepreneurship. Your classes* were the best decisions I made in university.

To Huxley, Scruffy, and all my furry friends
– For your unconditional love, loyalty, and plethora of smiles, I thank you.

And finally, to my love, Shveta *– You give me somewhere to lean when I feel weakest and you restore my strength when I feel down. I love you more than you can imagine, and I am grateful for being fortunate enough to have crossed paths with you. You encourage me every single day. Thank you.*

TABLE OF CONTENTS

◆ ◆ ◆

YOUR FREE GIFT

❖ ❖ ❖

Welcome! I'm glad you have picked up this book – it means a lot!

As a show of thanks, I created a **free** workbook called, "Five Practice Tips That Will Bring Your Nonverbal Communication to the Next Level: Without Having to Talk to New People!"

This is filled with exercises I practiced when I first started learning to communicate that helped me get over the initial barrier of trying to figure out how to enhance my verbal communication.

Want to really sell what you are saying?

Get your copy at www.galhad.com!

What You Will Get

1. A simple practice curriculum designed to help you absorb as much information as possible!
2. Basic tips to improve various nonverbal communication elements such as posture, eye contact, and more!
3. A workbook with simple assignments to help you

pick up on what powerful nonverbal communication looks like!

Download your copy at www.galhad.com!

FOREWORD

◆ ◆ ◆

I'm going to share a secret with you: I used to not be able to talk to anyone.

Not my friends.

Not girls.

Not even my family.

Think about that—being so shy that you cannot even hold a conversation with your own mother (who, by the way, makes a mean bowl of guacamole).

Let me tell you a story that I think sums up my situation perfectly.

When I was a kid, I spent most of my childhood growing up just outside of Reading, Pennsylvania. Back then I was an avid gamer and a huge fan of the Final Fantasy series. I wanted to work for Square Enix, the company that made those games.

Unfortunately, being so engrossed in video games stunted my interpersonal skills and prevented me from having many friends. When I graduated from high school, my dream was to be a concept artist for Square Enix, and I needed to figure out what college would give me the best shot at fulfilling my aspirations.

Square Enix employed top-of-the-line artists. Going to a second-rate university would never land me a spot working for them. I needed to go to the best art school to even stand a chance. At the time, Virginia Commonwealth University was ranked as the top public art school in the United States, and it was located in the city of Richmond, Virginia—a bit of a hike from Reading. The thought of moving so far from home was utterly terrifying.

But it was also an opportunity.

I had a chance to start fresh, meet new people, and make friends. As I grew up, I was alone most of the time. I had always wanted to talk to the other kids at school, flirt with girls in my class, and know how to answer when my family asked me, "How was your day?"—but I never knew what to say. The thought of how long I had lived like this tore me to pieces. I knew that this move would mark a much-needed change in my life and I had to take it. I packed my bags, said goodbye to my hometown, and headed south.

Once in Richmond, I immediately started going out to meet people. Unfortunately, as I went to malls, parks, parties, and other social events and venues, I began to realize something about myself that I had never known.

I was not just shy—I was afraid!

Sound familiar? Perhaps you feel this way too. If I could describe it, it is the tension in your neck, the blur in your vision, and the cold gripping your heart happening all at once. It feels like death.

And when did I feel it?

Every time I wanted to talk to someone but was stopped short by the thought, "I don't know what to say!"

If I wanted to talk to somebody who was walking with a group of other people, you could forget about it!

It all felt horrible! I felt alone in the world. Everyone else at those social venues was talking, flirting, bonding—and there I was, alone.

However, after trying for months on end with little to no success, I had a revelation. I realized something that would help me converse masterfully and aid me in landing any job I interviewed for, talking to women, and having a relationship with my family.

I was sitting in my room one day after a frustrating day of "socializing" and started playing my guitar while composing a new song. As I was referring to music theory and researching frameworks that helped composers write pieces, I began to think about how I would have never been able to learn music if all I thought it was comprised of was random notes. How thankful I was (and still am) that this art has theories and frameworks that support the reasoning behind a piece of music sounding the way it does. I laughed to myself because I wondered how easy talking with people would be if the art of conversation had frameworks, too.

And that is when it hit me.

What if conversations were built on frameworks that could be strategically applied to any topic?

I will repeat ...

What if conversations were built on frameworks that could be strategically applied to any topic?

It was one of those harmonious eureka moments when everything in the world seems to come together and make sense. This realization was the turning point in my view of conversation that took me from bedroom stowaway to being able to talk about anything with anyone—family members, friends, random strangers, CEOs, celebrity martial artists, and more!

What I will show you in this book are frameworks that I call "strategic conversation frameworks," or SCFs. From getting past small talk to gaining trust in strangers, I cover the whole gamut in these easy-to-use frameworks that anyone can master.

After developing and implementing these SCFs, not only did I manage to make new friends and develop the relationships I longed for in my life, I also successfully interviewed my way into having numerous job offers before I graduated university, met and dated incredible women, and started my first business with a healthy number of clients.

I had finally found secrets that worked, and I am excited to share them with you in this book.

If you are sick of feeling left out and not knowing what to say, and you want to change that, this book is for you.

If you want to make connections, boost your confidence, prepare for that interview, or talk to that special person you have always been too afraid to converse with, this book is for you.

If you want to see conversation not as some

random words but as something structured and easy to engage in, this book is for you.

These SCFs will turn you into a conversation-alist who will know what to say and be able to talk to anyone about anything.

So, without further ado, let's get started in making you the conversationalist you were always meant to be!

To your success,

Alixander

HOW TO USE
THIS BOOK

◆ ◆ ◆

I designed this book with a specific method to allow you to absorb as much information as possible. The method is as follows:

1. At the back of this book you will find a Certificate of Completion. Fill out the "Start Date" section.

2. Read Part I: Elements of Communication in order. It will give you a baseline understanding of theory to help you think about communication with a different perspective.

3. Read Part II: Eleven Strategic Conversation Frameworks in order. Each chapter includes an SCF's name, a brief description of it, its benefits, when to use it, how to use it, a sample script, commentary and tips, and a series of challenges. Save the challenges for the second read-through.

4. Complete the worksheets on each SCF at the end of the book, referring back to the corresponding chapters as needed.
5. Read through the SCFs again and complete the easy challenges.
6. Read through the SCFs once more and complete the medium challenges.
7. Read through the SCFs one last time and complete the hard challenges.
8. When you've done all these things, revisit the Certificate of Completion on the final page and fill out the "Date Completed" section.
9. Print out your Certificate of Completion.

You will notice that many of the challenges require you to converse with a friend or family member. Find a supportive influence in your life and/or somebody looking to improve their conversational skills and complete this book together.

Finally, a brief overview of a few discussions that I have had on the topic of conversation that are worth mentioning:

First, on nonverbal communication: Many people focus entirely on what to say without thinking at all about their nonverbal delivery. I believe this subject deserves a book dedicated to it, and I plan to write about it in the future. With that said, the main objective of this book is to pick out what words to say and topics to discuss and learn how to tie them into your conversations.

Second, on wit and humor: Like nonverbal communication, I find that wit and humor are topics worthy of discussion in their own right. However, I believe that these aspects of speech work best when the speaker has a solid foundation in the art of conversation.

Third, and finally, on the skills of others: In my experience of learning to speak, there have been times when, for the life of me, I could not get another person to respond in a manner that drives conversation. For a long time, I thought it was because I was not a good enough conversationalist.

However, a lesson I had to remember was that conversation is not a one-person activity; it requires input from the other party. While in this book I cover ways to nudge your conversation partner to speak in ways that keep the discussion going, the fact is that you do not have control over what they say and how they act. In short, sometimes people are either not in the mood to talk or simply have not refined their skills in conversation. Neither is something you are responsible for and therefore you should not blame yourself.

Follow the curriculum outlined above and you will achieve noticeable improvement in your conversation skills!

If you are curious about learning and mastering other aspects of conversation, visit www.galhad.com to check for new materials and updates!

PART I

Elements of Communication

CHAPTER I:

Cars Are Freaking Complicated

Picture this: You are driving down the road and all of a sudden you hear an incessant thunking from under the hood of your car. It sounds like your vehicle is going to die on the spot. Oh boy . . .

You pull over to the side of the road and despite having *no* mechanical experience, you decide to pop open your hood and see if you can figure out what the heck is wrong. After you lift the hood, you look at what's inside and the first thought that comes to your mind is probably something like this . . .

Cars are freaking complicated.

Despite driving one every day can you honestly say you know everything about how your vehicle works? Probably not. No worries though—most people don't! We know how to drive it, but when it comes to all the elements that make up a vehicle, we don't know how they tie together. Anybody can drive down the road, but how many people know enough about their suspension to hit a turn just right and maintain the maximum amount of speed and momentum to enhance their gas mileage?

Did that last sentence make your head spin? Good—because it illustrates this point:

There are things in our lives that we use so frequently that we don't even think about how they work.

Communication, for many of us, is one of these things.

I'm sure you have heard or had successful conversations in your life, but do you know the elements that made those conversations so easy going? Perhaps you have realized that your communication methods are "breaking down," so to speak, and you are "opening the hood" to look at the elements that make a conversation.

We are surrounded by communication every single day. Conversations with friends and watching the news are just a couple of forms in which communication can be manifested. It is so ubiquitous that we as individuals have never recognized the need to break it down into its elements to analyze them. How many people sit down and analyze an interview, a podcast, or even a conversation they had with their friends or family after the fact? My guess is, not many.

The few people who recognize their need to improve their conversation skills and look for ways to identify patterns are often given prepackaged phrases to memorize and pull out for particular situations. This is a relatively ineffective way of improving one's conversations because of the very nature of discourse. Communication can go in any direction!

Instead of using raw memorization of phrases, what if we looked at conversation in the form of theoretical frameworks?

To explain in a metaphorical sense, when you learned to add, did you memorize "1+1=2," "2+1=3," "3+1=4," and so on? Of course not! If you had, your knowledge of arithmetic would be incredibly limited and the effort to memorize those equations would have eaten up all your time. Instead, you learned the number line and what direction to count depending on whether you were adding or subtracting, how the numbers related, and other frameworks that could be universally applied to any equation.

That is how this book is going to approach the subject of conversation.

I'm not here to give you a prescribed line to say to someone while you are waiting in line at the theatre to see the next Spiderman movie and another totally different line to say to that cute man or woman waiting behind you at Starbucks.

I'm here to help you figure out what to say to anyone anywhere.

Imagine that instead of worrying about what to say in a particular situation, you can recognize elements and start piecing them together on the fly. It makes the task of conversation much easier to grasp.

In this part of the book, I will introduce you to the elements of communication. In the next part we will explore simple frameworks that you can use in *any* conversation, no matter the topic. Finally, we will look at more in-depth examples of how these elements and frameworks are utilized.

First, we must address the distinction between communication and conversation.

According to Merriam–Webster, the definitions of the two are as follows:

Communication: A process by which information is exchanged between individuals through a common system of symbols, signs, or behavior.

Conversation: Oral exchange of sentiments, observations, opinions, or ideas.

In short, the difference is that communication is the sharing of information by any means, whereas conversation is a discussion. I make this distinction for two reasons: one, I will be using both of these terms frequently in this book, and two, the SCFs that I will be providing in the second part of this book are designed specifically for verbal conversation.

Got it? Great!

Next, let's look at the elements we will be covering in this part of the book.

Verbal and nonverbal communication – What we say and how we say it

Medium – The method we choose to communicate

Context – The context of the communication

Types of communication – The flow and objective of the conversation

The purpose of overviewing these elements is to give you a new way of thinking about how communication is formed. We will dig deep enough to give you a working knowledge of how these elements play with each other in communication in general so that when you reach Part II: Eleven Strategic Conversation Frameworks, you will be able to envision how each of the SCFs can be applied or limited by various conversations.

A few things I would like to disclose before we get into the nitty-gritty:

This is NOT a book written specifically on how to negotiate.

This is NOT a book written specifically on persuasion.

This is NOT a book written specifically for dating, public speaking, or any other type of conversation (which we will touch on later).

This IS a book that will give you baseline knowledge that will help you in each of these endeavors instead of focusing on a specific area. Think of this as a 101 course.

Excited? Then let's get to it!

CHAPTER II:

*Nonverbal and Verbal
Communication*

Nonverbal Communication

The first elements of conversation we will observe are nonverbal and verbal communication. Although the SCFs presented in Part II are designed for verbal communication specifically, nonverbal communication needs to be touched on. Without it, we may as well sound like Microsoft Sam, and that does not make for good communication!

With that said, let's touch briefly on non-verbal communication. After all, it communicates more to those you are conversing with than your actual words do.

How can that be?

Think about how long humans and our ancestors have been on this earth. For hundreds of thousands of years, we relied solely on nonverbal communication that gradually became more sophisticated as our brains evolved (NTU).

Our first records of written language are from only around 5,000 years ago (Jackendoff).

We as a species managed to survive and thrive in the midst of the wrath of nature and join together because of the messages we could only grunt to each other. Through the coldest winters, hottest summers, natural disasters, and encounters with predators, we survived the vast majority of our existence with very primitive means of communicating.

That's pretty cool if you ask me.

It also makes sense that nonverbal communication speaks volumes despite not making a sound! To understand it further, we need to think about how it serves one of four purposes in tandem with your verbal communications (Wertheim 3):

Complementing: Matching what you say on purpose

Suggesting: Not matching what you say on purpose

Contradicting: Not matching what you say by accident

Substituting: Nonverbal replaces verbal

communication

Let's dive deeper into each of these.

Complementing: Matching What You Say on Purpose

Imagine that you are walking down the street and you hear your name being called. You turn around and it's your best friend behind you— big smile, waving, and saying hello. How awesome —you ran into a friendly face!

Your friend's nonverbal smiling and waving reinforced their verbal calling of your name and saying hello.

Suggesting: Not Matching What You Say on Purpose

We all know someone who is a great flirt. Chances are they are a master at suggestive non-verbal communication. Most of the time, they can flirt with someone in front of a whole group of people! You can sense it, and everybody knows it's going on, but to put it into tangible terms is a bit difficult.

What they are saying seems innocent

enough. After all, they are talking with that person while spending time with the rest of the group. But there is more going on ... The eye contact? The way they talk? How do you put your finger on it?

Nine times out of ten, what the two flirters are saying to each other doesn't stray too much from the group conversation. However, they *suggest* intimacy to one another through their nonverbal communication and build sexual tension. Purely intentional—and very slick!

Be it flirting, telling someone to do something nicely, or sarcasm, a suggestive nonverbal is extremely effective. This is because we can easily track what others are saying but have a hard time pinning down nonverbal communication, which creates a dissonance between what we hear and what we feel.

Contradicting: Not Matching What You Say by Accident

On the opposite side of complementary and suggestive nonverbal communication is contradicting. For the sake of example, let's juxtapose the successful flirt we previously talked about with somebody not so successful.

Imagine a man seeing a beautiful woman at the grocery store. He musters his courage to go talk to her. As he approaches, he is riddled with anxiety. This makes every compliment he gives and every move he makes unnerving to the woman. If you were to read his words on paper, you would find them sweet. However, when paired with his contradicting nonverbal communication, shaky demeanor, lack of eye contact, and other nonverbal cues, the words he says come across as awkward to the woman.

Keep in mind that this is not the only plausible situation. This can happen to women, men, and anybody who is interested in somebody else or wants to communicate a message. If you are not aware of your nonverbal communication you risk detracting from your message!

Unlike suggestive communication, being unaware of or unable to control how our nonverbal cues are sending a different message than what we are saying is very off-putting to others.

Substituting: Nonverbal Replaces Verbal Communication

Finally, nonverbal communication also has the ability to communicate by itself, without the assistance of verbal cues.

Waving your hand means hello or goodbye. You can tell if somebody is angry or happy by their expression alone. These are basic examples of substituting nonverbal communication.

Now that we understand how nonverbal communication interacts with verbal communication, let's look at the list of nonverbal communication methods and a brief description of each (Blatner):

Facial expressions – Self–explanatory. Are you smiling? Frowning? ...

Posture – How you hold your body. Are you standing tall? Slouching? ...

Gestures – How you move your body. Are you waving your arms? Walking the stage? ...

Eye contact – How you maintain and/or break your gaze. Are you looking at someone? Looking away? ...

Touch – How you make physical contact with someone. Are you patting them on the back? Brushing their hair? ...

Space – How far you are from someone. Are you far away? Close? ...

Pace – How fast or slow you talk. Are you zipping through your words? Pausing? ...

Tone – How you say your words to infer a certain meaning. Are you sincere? Sarcastic? . . .

Props – How you use objects to communicate. Are you twirling a pencil out of boredom? . . .

Reaction – How you respond, voluntarily or involuntarily, to communication. Are you sweating? Is your heart thumping? . . .

Keep these in mind when you communicate with others. Although nonverbal communication is not the primary focus of the SCFs, being aware of and using it effectively will have an immensely positive effect on your conversations. I cannot highlight enough how important this is when it comes to being a successful communicator!

Now that we have a baseline knowledge of nonverbal communication, let's look at verbal communication. However, if you want to dive more into the topic, subscribe at www.galhad.com for a copy of my free worksheet *"5 Simple Practice Tips That Will Bring Your Nonverbal Communication to the Next Level – Without Having to Talk to New People!"*

Verbal Communication

The entire second part of this book is going to be focused on verbal communication. There are two modes of verbal communication: written and spoken. Fortunately, they are very closely related, which allows a book to be a phenomenal method of learning spoken communication—the written word is easily translatable into spoken language. Let's take a look at a few ways these methods manifest themselves.

Written

Written communication is via any medium where the words are processed by sight. This includes mail, email, and texts, as well as other forms.

Spoken

Spoken communication is via any medium where the words are processed by sound. This includes face-to-face conversation, speeches, and even radio, to name a few.

Much like the elements of nonverbal communication, verbal communication has *topics* that drive the communication in various directions. Each topic has various characteristics that can lead into other topics.

When it comes to conversation, the success of the verbal aspect depends on the discovery and navigation of these topics. Again, this is what the entire second part of this book will be dedicated to uncovering!

CHAPTER III:

Medium of Communication

The next element to focus on is the medium we use to communicate. The message we convey is hugely affected by the medium we use. Think about this scenario:

Have you ever received a text and weren't sure how to take the message? Perhaps you wanted to make plans for the weekend with a friend. You suggest going to see a movie and they text you "Sure."

"Sure"? As in, sure, they would like to go? Or sure, they just want me to stop talking? Is it a good sure? A bad sure? What does "sure" mean?

Imagine that you have this interaction in person. You can pick up on their nonverbal cues and tell if they are genuinely interested. A "sure" with a nod would be a definite yes! A sure with an eye roll—probably not so much.

The medium of communication we use will either enhance or detract from our ability to use certain verbal or nonverbal techniques!

There is a reason that emojis have become so popular for texting: they act as a substitute for the nonverbal cues absent from this specific medium! Let's briefly go back to the previous example. You are suggesting plans for the weekend to your friend via text and bring up going to the movies. You receive one of the following responses:

"Sure :)"

"Sure."

"Sure –_–"

They signal very different reactions to the idea (positive, neutral, and negative, respectively).

Medium is something that should be considered when delivering your message and should be a factor in determining the words you choose to communicate. Unfortunately, this is largely overlooked and leads to numerous instances of miscommunication. To combat this, let's take a look at the various types of mediums used to communicate and how they can affect your communication.

First, we need to understand that a medium is divided into two areas: in–person and remote.

In–person

Speaking face to face—simple!

Pros:

- You can communicate a variety of emotions and messages by combining verbal and non-verbal communication elements on the spot.
- Deep connections and lasting relationships are best made this way.

Cons:

- Your messaging in most types of communication must be on the spot and therefore has a steeper learning curve.

Remote

Communicating to somebody through one or many channels. This can be via email, an assistant, texting, or watching somebody on television, just to name a few. Remote communication can also be combined in a chain; for example, you receive a message from your boss via an email sent by their assistant. That chain would look like this:

1. The in–person interaction between your boss and his or her assistant.

2. The email sent from the assistant to you.

Pros:

· You can take the time to carefully craft your message.

· You can create repeatable templates to communicate in case you need to speak to masses of people.

Cons:

· Connections are more difficult to make.

· Messages can be subject to interpretation due to lack of nonverbal cues.

· Messages are subject to degrees of separation.

Note: **Degrees of Separation**

Degrees of separation are the number of channels a message has to traverse. In general, the more degrees of separation there are, the greater the chance a message has of being misinterpreted and the less chance a message has of being personal, effective, or inspirational. In short:

The more degrees of separation a message must

travel, the more it loses its potency and clarity!

This is the exact reason why the in-person medium is so effective—there are **zero** degrees of separation!

Receiving a "happy birthday" email from someone does not have nearly as much impact as being wished "happy birthday" in person—and can you imagine if they had their assistant email you a card?

It is for this reason that I had a rule when I did freelance artwork: I must *never* be more than two degrees of separation from my client. Any more than that and the message would get lost and nothing would get done properly!

It is worth repeating, so keep this little rule in mind when you communicate, as it will affect how you need to craft your message:

The more degrees of separation a message must travel, the more it loses its potency!

CHAPTER IV:

Context

Like medium, context is an element of communication that is often overlooked. Think about this scenario:

You are at a business networking event. People are dressed up, talking to each other, and looking for professionals with complementary skill sets and connections to help each other out. While you're talking with a group of people, it becomes noticeable that one of the attendees is using this networking event to meet some potential dates. The general mood of the event becomes a little awkward because the "flirter" is hitting on people very distastefully.

Using a business networking event to test your pickup skills is generally considered poor judgment. However, the key word here is "generally."

I'm not saying that networking events have never led to successful dates, nor am I saying that a date on Tinder has never led to meeting a guy who knows a guy who can get you a job. I simply want to bring up some questions worth analyzing:

1. Why are you more likely to land a job at a networking event and meet a date on Tinder?

2. Why is it possible to find the love of your life at a networking event and land a job through a contact you met on Tinder?

3. Since it's possible, why is it that you risk making people feel on edge when you try to find love while networking or get a job through a romantic contact?

I would argue that networking events and apps like Tinder are successful because they dial in the scope of expected communication. When you go to a business networking event, it's to meet other professionals and make connections. When you use Tinder, your purpose is usually to communicate romantic interests. Framing the context of your communication is one less variable you have to worry about.

However, those who are successful at framing the context themselves are able to achieve objectives that are outside the conventional context. This is why people can meet dates at networking events and land jobs through dating platforms.

Most people are neither aware of this fact nor interacting with other people who are open to possibilities outside of the conventional context. This is why communicating out of context poses a greater risk of failure.

Here are some ways that we frame the context in which we communicate:

- Type of communication – The number of speakers, their objectives
- Environment – The space in which communication is taking place
- Intensity – The energy or stress of the environment in which the communication is taking place
- Personality – The behavior and values of individual participants in communication

Type of Communication

We will dive deep in this in the next chapter, but for now understand that the number of speakers and their objectives will play a part in determining the context in which communication is shared. For example, a public speech on global warming and an open discussion on the same subject will be handled differently.

Environment

Why does environment have anything to do with how we communicate? Ask yourself these questions:

Would you have to project your voice differently if you were on stage in an auditorium speaking to a mass of people than if you were talking with a friend face-to-face in a coffee shop?

Would you speak to somebody differently in the middle of a nightclub than you would in your living room?

Are there times when you speak with your "inside voice" versus your "outside voice"?

The physical space you are in creates special contextual rules. I have noticed that most instruction on communication assumes a mild environment. You have probably heard that the best way to introduce yourself is to shake hands and exchange names. It would be shocking for a book to tell you, instead, to get so close to another person that you are touching and shout your name in their ear . . .

. . . until you take into account that this would be acceptable in the middle of a concert.

Environment changes the rules of communication.

Intensity

Back when I was in high school, one of my first jobs was in a restaurant. When the dinner rush hit, politeness between coworkers went out the window—we told each other loud and clear what to do, with no "pleases" or "thank yous." It was nothing personal; there just wasn't time for formalities or mistakes. Communication had to be crystal clear and efficient lest we mess up an order and set the whole kitchen back.

Flash forward—a short time after that, I was working in an office setting. I couldn't imagine speaking to one of my peers like I had in the kitchen. The intensity in the office was not as high as it had been in food service.

The stress and importance of time in a situation will affect how well your communication is received. Often people with great ideas to share are swept to the side because they're either too meek during high-intensity situations or too bossy during low-intensity situations.

Maintaining the perfect level of intensity is rarely natural for people. If you have trouble with being too commanding, passive, polite, or rude, learning to speak at different intensity levels to match any given situation will be invaluable to you as a leader and communicator.

Personality

The personality of those we communicate with will determine how we express our message. Various factors are in the realm of personality, including maturity, culture, and even an individual's expertise in a given field of study.

There is a reason we didn't get "the talk" until we were teenagers (thank goodness!).

We weren't mature enough!

Our culture defines a set of communication rules that we naturally abide by. They may violate another's cultural rules of communication, and this does not apply just to political borders. Think about how different generations prefer to communicate with one another—for example, with texts or face-to-face conversation!

Even expertise plays a huge role in how we communicate. Take two people with the same level of knowledge but in different fields. How much would a PhD in neuroscience know about Rococo? How much would a master painter know about the regions of the brain?

For a more relevant example, think back to your first day at a job or internship. Perhaps you became overwhelmed by the specialized jargon that many of the experienced employees used so cavalierly. If you were lucky enough to have coworkers help you catch on to the work, then perhaps you were lucky enough to find a more experienced coworker who could break down complex ideas and explain technical jargon to you, the new guy or gal.

Speaking consistently with the context and learning to frame the various factors that make up context in a way that favors your objectives will make your communication skills way more effective!

CHAPTER V:

Types of Communication

The final element of communication is the type of communication. This is a combination of the direction of communication and the objective of the participants.

Direction

Direction refers to how many people are engaging in conversation and its flow. Is it one person or group of people speaking to the masses? Is it a group of people speaking to each other? Is it a one-on-one conversation?

Objective

Objective refers to what the desired outcome

is of each participant in the communication. Is it sharing information? Is it persuading somebody to a point of view? Is it negotiating a better price?

Combinations of the various directions and objectives possible in communication create a virtually infinite number of types of communication. When a public speaker tries to persuade the masses, we call it persuasion. When two people try to persuade each other, we call it debate. When the multitude of possible objectives of persuasion are analyzed, we find more granular objectives, such as the following:

·   Manipulation – Getting people to do things for you.
·   Voting – Politicians do this all the time. They try to persuade the public to look at things from their point of view to win the vote.
·   Proof of innocence – Defending your innocence to protect your good name or avoid legal penalties.
·   Seduction – Self-explanatory!

. . . and these are just a few of many reasons to persuade others.

Imagine how multifaceted the objective of persuasion can be. Now, multiply that by various types of other objectives, such as information and entertainment. It becomes easy to see that when it comes to the type of communication, the way we decide to communicate must be based on strategy rather than technique.

In short, the manner in which you write and speak cannot be put into neat little buckets. Think of it like this . . .

How we speak to others and address our communication objectives will vary greatly depending on who we're talking to and what their objectives are. Consider the following example:

How do a public-school math teacher and a private math tutor approach presenting their curricula to their students?

The math teacher has to organize activities, structure classes, and communicate effectively to groups. The tutor has to prepare for face-to-face interaction and open dialogue with one person.

The math teacher has to teach and discipline to maintain order within the classroom.

The tutor may have to teach only a single student at a time.

Another example:

How do a CEO at a large company and a CEO at a startup lead their teams differently?

The large-company CEO may have to deliver their message to masses of employees at once. The startup CEO may be able to speak in-depth with each employee and share the information learned with other employees in open discussion.

The large-company CEO may have to summarize technical data with understandable jargon so that the entire company can have a sense of the direction the business is going. The startup CEO may only have to act as a communication liaison between two or more technical people.

While many people say that the types of communication are finite, I argue the opposite. The types of communication that exist are infinite, and rather than setting different rules for different types of communication that are applicable only in specific circumstances, we need strategies and principles.

In essence, dividing the countless types of communication into neat little subcategories such as persuasive speech, intense interrogation, flirting, interviewing, negotiating, and simply catching up with an old friend will limit your understanding greatly! The objectives within each of these categories can become much more granular.

Think about how the other elements of communication can be combined to strategically address each type of communication you encounter.

For example:

Let's look at Anderson Cooper versus Trevor Noah. Both communicate via television. Both are informative. However, you will notice that they talk about similar topics but combine elements in a different way.

Anderson Cooper adds complementary non-verbal cues to what he says verbally to present in a way that is more objective than Trevor Noah's approach, which uses a suggestive style with elements of humor. Cooper's target audience tends to be people over 35, while Noah's target audience is millennials.

The direction is the same and their objective of being informative is the same. Yet when you drill down on the objective of being informative, you realize that Cooper is trying to inform through objectivity while Noah is trying to inform via entertainment.

PART II

*Eleven Strategic
Conversation Frameworks*

THIS IS NOT A SCRIPT!

❖ ❖ ❖

You will notice as you read on that I have not provided you with prepackaged lines to pull out when the right situation presents itself.

As mentioned before, the paths down which a conversation can flow are far too numerous to measure and relying solely on canned phrases would make you a weak and robotic conversationalist.

The idea behind this book is twofold. Part one gave you the theory on what to keep an eye out for during conversation so you can develop a sensitivity to it over time. Part two introduces frameworks that can be applied to conversations no matter what the topic is or what path it goes down.

I designed these frameworks to be useful in as many everyday conversations as possible. They are not necessarily designed for negotiation, flirting, interviewing, or any specific type of communication, although mastering these frameworks will certainly play a part in helping you become a better negotiator, flirt, or interviewee. Instead they are a pragmatic baseline to help you view conversation in a new light.

The frameworks are for conversation, not all communication. They work best for discussion between two or a few people, as opposed to public speaking or communicating with the masses through television or radio. Like many things in this book, the latter deserve separate treatment. The purpose for introducing them in this book was to enhance your awareness of them.

Finally, as said before, due to the nature of writing and reading, these are frameworks that are centered around verbal communication. Nonverbal communication is not discussed as a framework here. Again, that topic deserves a book to itself.

Please check out www.galhad.com for books on these topics that are out now or will be coming out in the future!

Remember to review the "How to Use This Book" section to follow the step-by-step approach I have laid out for you to get this most out of this book!

Without further ado—let's get to work!

REAL CURIOSITY

SCF I

◆ ◆ ◆

Have you ever been engaged in a conversation with somebody but the only thing that runs through your mind is what should I say next?

Chances are that sounds familiar, since you're reading this book.

I remember that when I first started trying to hone my skills as a conversationalist, the only thing that was on my mind was figuring out my next line. I spent my time talking to people trying to anticipate what I needed to say to keep the conversation going. Yet conversations rarely went down the path I had prepared for. I was left speechless and scrambling mentally to find the next "right thing" to say.

The prepackaged lines that I picked up from articles, how-tos, and other sources were rarely useful.

No matter how many canned lines I had in my back pocket, I would never have the "perfect" thing to say due to the seemingly unpredictable nature of conversation. Through this realization, I began to discover that all the prepackaged lines I had learned were fundamentally flawed for this reason:

Conversation isn't about trying to predict the future —it is about responding to the present moment.

This led me to the conclusion that thinking what should I say next is also fundamentally flawed. When it comes to conversation, believing you can accurately predict what will happen next is an incredibly unrealistic expectation. Switching to the mindset of responding to the present moment raised a much better question.

"What do I hear now?"

This is where SCF I – Real Curiosity excels.

When I began switching my focus from what do I say next to what do I hear now, I realized that the people I was conversing with were handing me every conversational topic I could ask for on a silver platter! Even better than having an infinite number of conversational topics to draw from was this:

I actually learned incredible things from the people I spoke to.

From crazy hobbies to iron-clad opinion to personal stories, the wealth of knowledge and experience that each person harbored began to unfold at an unprecedented rate! I learned to become genuinely curious about other people no matter what the topic was.

What also made me love this SCF was that it required no speaking on my part! For a naturally shy person, becoming a better conversationalist without having to say a word was extremely attractive!

SCF I – Real Curiosity is the foundation for the other SCFs we will discuss. Take it to heart and it will take you far!

Description

Mindset that focuses on ingesting and interpreting information from the speaker.

Benefits

1. Obtain potential topics of conversation.

2. Service mindset – Many people who are not good conversationalists refrain from speaking to people because they feel that when they do, they are "dis–servicing" the other person (e.g., making them feel awkward, exposing them to uncomfortable conversation, wasting their time). Real curiosity means that you are genuinely interested in what the other person says. You are dedicating your time to learn more about them. By doing so, you are "servicing" them by giving them a genuine ear and empathy, which require no speaking skill. In short, being interested in another person can enhance your speaking, but is not dependent on it.

When to Use

Anytime during a conversation but especially when you are looking for things to say.

How to Use

Have you heard the adage "listen to understand, not to respond"? A good strategy is to gamify this SCF by seeing how many different things you can learn from what your conversation partners are saying.

Sample Script

While standing in line at a coffee shop you strike up a conversation with the person behind you

You – I've never been here before – what's your recommendation?

Friend – Um, let me think . . . I usually don't have a preference. As long as it has espresso in it.[1]

You – Caffeine kick? I guess you work a lot?

Friend – Yeah, I go to art school. Long hours of painting naked people.

You – That can't be all of it!

Friend – No, haha. But we have to study anatomy among other things. Painting people covers a lot of fundamentals. Color, light, proportion—everything. And considering I really want to illustrate comic books after school, being good at painting people is pretty important.[2]

Commentary and Tips

1. A great way to encourage the other speaker to continue the topic and let them know that you are listening is to paraphrase what they said.

2. This part is full of different topics to talk about—art fundamentals, color, light, proportion, and that your friend wants to illustrate comic books.

Challenge

Easy – Do this exercise with a friend or family member and learn three things.

Medium – Do this exercise with a friend or family member and learn five things.

Hard – Do this exercise with a friend or family member and learn seven things.

INTEREST/
AGREEMENT
OPENERS

SCF II

◆ ◆ ◆

Let's be real for a second.

We are all suckers for compliments. Compliments are one of the most powerful tools we have to make other people feel valued and useful!

Unfortunately for people who are on the shy side, giving compliments out of the blue may seem a little bit awkward. I can certainly attest to this.

Let's take a journey back in time to when I was a teenager. I remember sitting in the student lounge in my community college doing my homework when a woman my age brought in a box containing the Dance Dance Revolution video game, a couple of Dance Dance Revolution mats, a game console, and the wires that went with the game.

I was still a pretty big fan of video games at that time in my life, so when I saw this person bring the entire rig for playing this game into school, I had only one thought: This woman is cool and I need to talk to her.

Unfortunately, I had barely begun honing my social skills. What was I going to say to break the ice? I was too shy to give her a direct compliment, and every other way to open a conversation seemed stupid to me.

This is where the beauty of SCF II – Interest/Agreement Openers appears.

It is a perfect marriage of a subtle compliment wrapped in a question of intrigue.

When I began a conversation by attempting to build a bridge of commonality, I felt a lot more comfortable breaking the ice. In a sense, by initiating the offer of building a relationship through the establishment of common ground, my first impression on people was that of connection. Consider the ever-growing hostility that each of us faces because of political, religious, and other personal beliefs.

It's easy to see why showing your conversation partner that you "come in peace" can lower a lot of their barriers and open the way for meaningful connections. After all, we are less hesitant to share more of ourselves with those who are similar to us.

SCF II – Interest/Agreement Openers is a way to set the context of positive discussion for the conversation.

◆ ◆ ◆

Description

Begin a sentence or interrogative with a phrase indicating interest or agreement.

Benefits

By turning common questions into subtle commands or indicators, you will create a stronger prompt for a response from those you are talking to.

When to Use

This is an effective opener. It can be used to switch or dig deeper into a conversational topic.

How to Use

Place an interest or agreement phrase (I would like to, I'd love to, I'm interested in, I feel like we agree) in front of an interrogative (who, what, where, etc.) to turn a common question into a command that states interest.

Example:

Instead of "Where did you get those shoes?"

Say "I'd love to know where you got those shoes."

Instead of "You like rock and roll?"

Say "I feel like we agree that rock and roll beats rap."

Sample Script

You – I'd like to know where you got that video-game. It's one of my favorites![1]

Person – Oh, thanks! I actually got it as a gift from my best friend.

Commentary and Tips

1. "I'd like to know where you got that video-game" replaces "Where did you get that video-game?" By turning the original question into a subtle command, you are more effectively prompting a response.

Tip: The agreement opener will draw some disagreement. That's okay, as long as you do not focus on the disagreement. (For example, if they say they like rap better, don't press on with your opinion of why rock is preferable.) This is meant to be used as a playful assumption that either will be perceived positively as mutual agreement or give you a chance to learn something about them.

Challenge

Easy – Do this exercise three times with a friend or family member.

Medium – Do this exercise three times with different people.

Hard – Do this exercise three times with different people in twenty-four hours.

KEEP IT OPEN

SCF III

❖ ❖ ❖

There are many things I like: sunny days, windy beaches, dogs, scotch, and supreme pizza, to name a few.

There are also many things I dislike: cold rain, stepping on seashell fragments, cockroaches, tequila, plain cheese pizza, and the letter "k" as a response to a text. For example:

"Want to go to the movies?"

"k"

Drives me nuts!

I am willing to bet that being on the receiving

end of "k" makes you a little frustrated, too.

One-word answers are nearly impossible to work with if you are not prepared to deal with them! However, when I realized I actually had control over the quality of the responses I received, I was thrilled!

Before I began using SCF III – Keep it Open, my natural tendency was to ask questions that prompted a yes or no response. If I was going to get a one-word answer, then I wanted it to have enough meat on it to give me a chance to propel the conversation.

The power of SCF III – Keep it Open lies in this fact:

Whether the response you receive is one word or a complete sentence, it will always have substance.

That's right! When I began asking open-ended questions, my conversation partners could not answer with words like "yes," "no," "sure," and "k." They had to give me substance! For example, using this SCF, a dialogue may look like this:

"What kind of movie would you be into seeing?"

This would prompt one of three types of answers.

1. A fulfilling answer: "I think I'd be down with seeing either a comedy or that thriller that just came out."

2. A substantial one-word answer: "Comedy."

3. An indecisive answer: "I don't know."

Don't worry, we will touch on how to deal with an indecisive answer in SCF X – Tridenting.

Give SCF III – Keep it Open a shot next time you want more than a one-word response!

Description

Using open-ended interrogatives to keep a conversation going.

Benefits

Open-ended questions make it awkward for your respondent to answer with simply "yes" or "no." They will put subtle pressure on them to divulge conversational topics to you.

When to Use

Anytime.

How to Use

Start questions with "who," "what," "when," "where," "why," "which," "how," or other words that cannot be answered easily with "yes" or "no."

Avoid starting questions with "did," "does," "are," or other words that prompt a "yes" or "no" answer.

Sample Script

Good:
You – Are you going out?
Man – Yes.

Better:
You – Where are you going?
Man – The basketball game.[1]

Commentary and Tips

1. By asking an open-ended question, you got information about a basketball game that you can talk about. It's much harder to talk about a yes or no.

Tip: Closed-ended questions do have their place. If you need definite answers, you should resort to these to eliminate any alternate interpretations. They can also be used once a stable rapport has been established with your conversation partner.

Challenge

Easy – Do this exercise three times with a friend or family member.

Medium – Do this exercise three times with strangers.

Hard – Do this exercise three times with three different strangers in twenty-four hours.

TOPICS: STORING AND REFERRING

SCF IV

◆ ◆ ◆

Awkward . . .

. . . silence.

I remember dreading networking events for this very reason. People would give me their elevator pitch, I would give mine, and then there would be awkward silence. Not the best first impression by any means!

What's worse is that it didn't make sense! Why was it that when I was at networking events, conventions, workshops, or any place where there was an abundance of very accomplished and famous people, I could not think of something to talk about when the conversation ran dry? There was obviously a lot these people had experienced and could share!

Fortunately, after I began using SCF I – Real Curiosity, I realized that the people I was conversing with provided me a wealth of conversational topics in addition to the one we were talking about! Without having to do anything except exercise a little bit of short-term memory, I could consistently store topics to transition to when our conversation ran out of steam.

Topics were abundant in conversation! As long as I could remember a few of them along the way I could transition back to them smoothly at any time!

Those elevator pitches people gave me weren't just empty scripts; they were chock-full of conversational topics that I could store in the back of my mind and refer to later in the conversation!

SCF IV – Topics: Storage and Referral is about understanding that what you learn from listening to people is more than just little tidbits of random information—it's also opportunities to carry the conversation forward!

Description

Collecting conversational topics to use when the subject being discussed runs its course.

Benefits

Nearly endless supply of things to say.

When to Use

Use this SCF at the beginning of a conversation and when you run out of nodes (next section). Rule of thumb: your first objective should be to store one to two extra topics as soon as you can and keep that many in the back of your mind to jump to when a conversational topic runs dry.

How to Use

Use SCF I — Real Curiosity to search for topics to store. When a conversation runs dry, jump to another topic.

Sample Script

Beginning of conversation

You – Hi. I'm [your name]. Nice to meet you.

Jake – Hey there. Nice to meet you. I'm Jake.

You – Hi Jake, where are you headed to?

Jake – I'm actually making a pit stop up the block and then headed to work.[1]

Later in conversation

Jake – . . . and that's more or less how I got into accounting.2

You – Wow; who would have thought! By the way, you mentioned earlier that you're making a pit stop up the block. I'm guessing you're grabbing lunch at this hour?3

Jake – I wish! No, I'm actually headed there to shop for some treats. It's my dog's birthday tomorrow.

You – You have a dog? I'd love to know more about him. Name? Breed?

Commentary and Tips

1. Notice the two topics given in this sentence. The first is the pit stop and the second is work. You talk about work and store the pit stop.

2. You choose to talk about work but later in the conversation the topic runs dry.

3. You refer to the pit stop, which leads to multiple other topics to store and refer to later, such as what kind of shop Jake is heading to and his dog.

Challenge

Easy – In a conversation, store two topics and refer to at least one of them.

Medium – In a conversation, store two topics and refer to at least one of them. Then store a replacement topic.

Hard – In a conversation, store two topics and refer to at least one of them. Then store a replacement topic. Do this twice.

TOPICS: NODES

SCF V

When I was in college, I worked a lot with 3D modeling programs to create characters, environments, props, and other objects for games and movies. One program I used was Maya. Within it was a feature that paralleled conversation so effectively that it helped me exponentially increase the number of topics I could converse about even if the responses I was receiving from my conversation partners were minimal.

This feature is called Hypershade. It takes a material and separates its characteristics into nodes that you can add, subtract, and edit.

For example, let's say you wanted to make your material look metallic. You would give it nodes for color, shininess, smoothness, transparency, reflectiveness, and more!

What does this have to do with talking to other people?

Think about it like this:

Every topic you can possible converse about has "nodes" that are hidden within it. The topic of dogs can have nodes like size, weight, breed, and personality. In addition, dogs can itself be a node of something broader, such as animals or pets.

SCF V – Topics: Nodes leverage the individual characteristics of topics to expand potential points to speak about.

What makes me appreciate this SCF is that it is especially effective if you or your conversation partner is particularly shy. For people who may have a difficult time picking up on new topics during a conversation, having the ability to expand a topic to its full worth is an invaluable skill to have.

SCF V – Topics: Nodes will enhance your sensitivity to all things applicable to a particular conversational topic.

Description

Extrapolating extra topics from the characteristics of a single topic.

Benefits

Limitless conversational topics that flow easily together.

When to Use

Anytime your current topic runs dry or if you see a chance to amplify (next section) a similar topic or have to mute (explained later) the current topic.

How to Use

Take a topic and pull as many characteristics as you can from it. For example, if somebody talks about the topic of their love of Stanley Kubrik films, you can extrapolate the following:

Stanley Kubrik, the director
Various films by Kubrik; e.g., The Shining, 2001: A Space Odyssey

From these you can look at genre, actors, etc. and go further from there.
Film production
Visual art
... and much more.

Sample Script

You – What kind of movies are you into?[1]

Man – I love anything by Stanley Kubrik.[2]

You – I love The Shining; it's one of my favorites![3]

Man – The Shining is a great one. Can you believe they almost cast Robin Williams to play the lead?[4]

Commentary and Tips

1. The topic starts off as movies.

2. The man speaks about the node of movie dir-

ectors, specifically, Stanley Kubrik.

3. You look at the nodes associated with Kubrik and float back to movies. You choose his work The Shining.

4. Finally, from among The Shining's nodes, the man chooses actors associated with that film and talks about Robin Williams.

Challenge

Easy – In a conversation, store two nodes and refer to at least one of them.

Medium – In a conversation, store two nodes and refer to at least one of them. Then store a replacement topic.

Hard – In a conversation, store two nodes and refer to at least one of them. Then store a replacement topic. Do this twice.

TOPICS: AMPLIFICATION

SCF VI

◆ ◆ ◆

Who would rather spend your time with, a person who builds upon your point of view or a person who refutes everything you say?

Whether we choose to admit it or not, we like being around people who agree with us more than we do people who don't. That's not to say that we don't like a healthy debate! However, I was arguably the world's biggest player of the devil's advocate and my ability to make connections with others suffered because of it.

Constantly playing devil's advocate or even focusing too much on your own agenda is not the best way to con-

nect with people.

Perfect example:

Flash back to when I was in my early twenties and living in Virginia. I began teaching guitar on the side for a little extra cash. I had studied music and played guitar for almost ten years and I was very confident in my abilities as a musician. However, the transition into teaching was a bit trickier than I had imagined it would be.

I remember having a hard time instructing one of my first students, who was a twelve-year-old boy. I wanted to teach him everything in order to make him as good of a musician as possible. I tried showing him theory, transcription, ear training, strict guitar playing techniques, and more. However, every week when we met for his private lesson, I could tell that he had not been practicing.

During one of the check-in meetings I had with him and his parents, I asked what his initial reason was for deciding to pick up the instrument. He sheepishly looked down to the floor—it was clear that he was embarrassed about something.

It was an innocent question. There could only be one thing a twelve-year-old boy would be afraid to admit in front of his guitar teacher and mother.

"Dude. You doing this for the ladies?" I asked.

He gave a little shrug.

"All good, my man. Me too." I smiled.

I restructured the lessons to target songs that would be better for wooing, so to speak. We also began lessons with tales of my many attempts to use my guitar playing to impress women. Unfortunately for me, being a progressive metal guitarist did not tend to leave ladies head over heels.

It was when I shared our common ground of playing guitar to meet girls with my student that I saw his desire and ability to play significantly increase.

SCF VI – Topics: Amplification highlights what we share. It is in common ground where we lay the strongest foundations for a connection.

Description

Highlighting mutual interest in a particular topic.

Benefits

People like being around those who are like them. By focusing on topics where there is mutual interest, you are showing the person you're talking to that the two of you are alike.

When to Use

Anytime there is a topic of mutual interest.

How to Use

When the person you're talking to shows and/or expresses interest in a topic, focus on that topic.

Sample Script

You – When I was in high school, I played football. My dream was to play for the Pittsburgh Steelers.

Man – You're a Steelers fan? I've rooted for them my entire life![1]

You – Yeah, I'm a Steelers fan! Have you ever been to a game?[2]

Commentary and Tips

1. They recognize that you like the Steelers and mention their interest.

2. You switch the topic from football in general to the Steelers specifically because your partner expressed interest in that particular topic.

Challenge

Easy – Find a topic to amplify in a conversation with a friend or family member.

Medium – Find a topic to amplify in a conversation with a stranger.

Hard – Find two topics to amplify in a conversation with a stranger.

TOPICS: MUTING

SCF VII

Imagine that you are in the midst of a conversation and it takes a turn for the worse. You are still talking about a topic that you and the other person clearly have polar-opposite views on, and this is not the most tactful time for debate. It's not that you want to stay on this topic.

It's just that you have NOTHING else to say!

Naturally you continue talking about that topic for no reason other than to keep the conversation going in the desperate hope that it will turn around. Unfortunately, nine times out of ten, you will just isolate yourself from the other person even more.

I'll be frank—I used to do this all the time.

Be it talking about a recent death in the family, discussing opposing opinions, or divulging my favorite sports team to the wrong crowd, I had a bad habit of not knowing how to switch topics in a tasteful way. SCF VII – Topics: Muting excels at this objective because of its combination of empathy and smooth transition to a new topic via other SCF techniques.

As important as it is to establish a connection with another person, it is equally important not to destroy one.

The unfortunate fact of the matter is that when jumping from topic to topic, the risk of landing on a sore subject is high. Instead of trying to avoid tough conversations by holding back on potentially worthwhile topics, learn to put out the fires if they ever come up!

SCF VII –Topics: Muting allows us to preserve the connection we have while fearlessly exploring new territory for conversational topics.

◆ ◆ ◆

Description

This is the opposite of amplification. Muting is switching topics when a conversation is highlighting the differences between you and the other person.

Benefits

Just as we like being around those who are similar to us, we tend to be more reserved around people who are not like us or whom we associate with negative feelings.

When to Use

Whenever a conversation is moving toward disagreement or getting too somber too fast.

How to Use

Once you sense a topic is a topic of opposition, use SCF IV — Topics: Storing and Referring and SCF V — Topics: Nodes to change topics smoothly to a new topic. Here is an effective formula for doing so:

Empathy statement –> New topic transition –> New topic

Sample Script

You – Your cat sounds adorable! Speaking of pets, you should meet my dog. He goes crazy over frozen bananas.[1]

Woman – Yeah . . . I'm sure he's nice but I'm a bit scared of dogs. I was attacked when I was really little.[2]

You – I can't even imagine what that was like! Actually, when I was really little, I was more of a cat person. I had a cat named Allison that I was really close to. She was a bit chubby. That was partly my doing.[3]

Commentary and Tips

1. You take the topic of pets and use it as an opportunity to dig deeper into a more personal conversation, specifically about your dog.

2. Unfortunately, your partner had a traumatizing experience with dogs in their youth.

3. You offer empathy—"I can't even imagine what that was like"—and, using the amplification of

"really little," transition back into a topic, cats, that your partner was passionate about. You then offer a statement about your cat to solidify the transition.

Tip: Disagreement can often drive a conversation. Tension and debate will help you establish yourself as a strong person from the perspective of your conversation partner. However, these should be reserved for only a few instances:

1. Values, morals, and ethics – Agreeing in a way that violates your values, morals, or ethics will cause you to be perceived as a pushover. While an open mind is important, be sure to think before blindly throwing these traits of yours away for the sake of approval from another person. Most likely you will earn no respect from them.

2. Knowing when to disagree to drive a conversation forward generally takes a little more intuition if it is not in the realm of debate. My rule of thumb: try to find at least two topics to amplify before muting a topic.

3. Weighing the likely outcomes of muting certain topics versus speaking about them on the fly is an acquired skill that comes naturally with practice. With that said, if you feel tension in choosing which option to go with, ask yourself, first, if the relationship with the person is more or less valuable than the conversation. Then decide whether the re-

lationship with the person can withstand the level of disagreement you will be getting into if you choose to pursue the topic.

Challenge

Easy – During a conversation with a friend or family member, mute a topic when the conversation turns toward a disagreement.

Medium – Find a topic to mute in a conversation with a stranger.

Hard – Mute a conversational taboo (politics, religion, belief-based topics) with a conversational partner. This is a great challenge for Thanksgiving! (I'm kidding—or am I?)

TOPICS: WEAVING

◆ ◆ ◆

"So . . . how about this weather?"

Small talk. This is what I despised most when I disliked conversation. Even if I knew how to introduce myself or make an observation to start a conversation, I was always afraid of the dreaded small talk that was soon to follow.

However, after the discovery of various other SCFs such as SCF I – Real Curiosity and SCFs IV through VII – Topics, I began piecing together a framework that would help me dig deeper and have more meaningful conversations with friends and strangers alike.

As a matter of fact, I soon began to enjoy small talk because it was no longer the beginning and awkward final destination of a conversation. In fact, it was quite the opposite.

Small talk was merely a gateway to learning more deeply about a person.

SCF VIII – Topics: Weaving was what allowed me to navigate into deeper topics with my conversation partners. Pairing it with an understanding of the depth stages of a conversation, I could begin targeting what topics to speak about to drill quickly into an individual's most personal beliefs!

Once you can navigate topics successfully, weave them together with a targeted objective of conversing more deeply to truly learn the most from your conversational partner.

Description

Chaining topics together to dig deeper into more substantial and private topics.

Benefits

Learn about a person on a much deeper level.

When to Use

As much as you can, given your partner's comfort level.

How to Use

Chain topics together to drive conversation to deeper levels. The levels of conversation, from the most superficial to the most private, are small talk (superficial subjects), fact disclosure (subjects like occupation or factual events), viewpoints and opinions (beliefs on subjects), and personal feelings (deeper emotions and beliefs) (Toastmasters International).

Sample Script

Sitting on the bench at a park

You – Gorgeous day! How are you doing today?[1]

Woman – I'm well. The flowers are finally starting to bloom, so that's nice.[2]

You – What kind of flowers are your favorite?

Woman – Well, I actually don't know. I'm not really that big into them. I just think they're pretty.[3]

You – Me too. Sometimes it's just nice to appreciate things as they come. What do you think?

Woman – Yeah, it's too stressful to try to be an expert on everything! I like just taking things at face value. Does that seem shallow? *laughs*[4]

You – Not at all! I feel the same way. Seems like we agree that there's a lot of pressure to be perfect at everything—but that's no way to enjoy life.

Woman – Right. I run into that problem so much with my coworkers and it just blows my mind how people go through life being so uptight about perfecting everything![5]

Commentary and Tips

1. Simple small talk about the day.
2. She states a fact—that the flowers are blooming.
3. After you look for an opinion on flowers, she shares her opinion that she just likes things that are

pretty.

4. Now she is expressing a personal belief about a general value of hers—that sometimes it's nice to just take things at face value.

5. Since you validated her values, she divulges more information about them; e.g., that people she works with violate her beliefs through their actions and they seem miserable.

Challenge

Easy – Get to level 2 (Fact Disclosure) in a conversation with a stranger.

Medium – Get to level 3 (Viewpoints and Opinions) in a conversation with a stranger.

Hard – Get to level 4 (Personal Feelings) in a conversation with a stranger.

PLURAL ASKS

SCF IX

❖ ❖ ❖

Strap in because I am about to make an ice cream reference.

Imagine walking into an ice cream shop and going up to the big freezer with all the flavors. As you look inside you see there is only one flavor, vanilla. No strawberry, no chocolate, no pistachio. Just plain old vanilla.

What flavor would you order?

Yep. Plain old vanilla. (No hate from me, by the way. I love vanilla!)

How in the world does this tie into conversation? Let me explain.

I found that in my conversations, whenever I asked a question, I would prompt others to give me a single-word response. If I asked somebody what their favorite kind of music was, I would get answers like "rock," "rap," "country," etc.

Could I work off these answers in my conversation? Absolutely. However, I was cutting down the chances of finding a topic the two of us could really connect on. How I was asking my questions suggested to them that I was looking for a simple answer.

I was prompting people to give me vanilla and only vanilla. I wanted more topics—more "flavors"—to choose from.

Fortunately, the solution was astonishingly simple!

When I realized that the magic of SCF III – Keep it Open was that people responded in a way that was harmonious with what certain words demanded, I figured out that a similar tactic could be used to produce an array of responses instead of just one. Hence, SCF IX – Plural Asks was born.

Remember how in SCF III – Keep it Open, I explained that people find it awkward to respond "yes" or "no" to open-ended questions due to the interrogatives used? SCF IX – Plural Asks works in a similar fashion. Instead of using the singular form of a word, replace it with a plural.

"What is your favorite kind of music?" –> "What are your favorite kinds of music?"

"Where did you go on vacation?" –> "Wat were your most memorable vacations?"

"What flavor of ice cream do you prefer?" –> "What flavors of ice cream do you prefer?" (Mint chocolate chip, if you're curious.)

A simple but powerful tool, SCF IX – Plural Asks will give you more topics to talk about without your having to think too much on how to receive those answers.

Use this SCF and enjoy all the flavors of conversation.

Description

Ask your question in plurals to prompt an array of responses.

Benefits

Singular asks tend to get singular responses, which provide limited topics. Plural asks prompt people to give various answers, which provide more conversational topics.

When to Use

Anytime you need to ask a question specifically for obtaining topics.

How to Use

Make the topic or subject of your question a plural.

Instead of, "What is your favorite restaurant?" which prompts a response like "Chipotle,"

ask "What are your favorite restaurants?" which prompts a response like "Chipotle, Qdoba, or Moe's" or a broader topic like "Mexican fast food."

Sample Script

You – I'm free next Thursday if you want to get together. What kind of places would you like to go to?

Friend – The new bar on 13th and Main would be cool to check out but I'm also down with our spot on 4th and Broad.[1]

Commentary and Tips

1. By asking questions in the plural, we will get an array of responses that we can follow up on.

Challenge

Easy – Use one time with a friend or family member.

Medium – Use one time with a stranger.

Hard – Use two times with a stranger.

TRIDENTING

SCF 10

◆ ◆ ◆

"Where do you want to eat?"

"I don't know."

Yep, we have all had this conversation. To be honest, before I learned how to be a better conversationalist I often resorted to this answer. It was comfortable and safe and didn't require me to risk saying something "stupid." It was my conversational trump card.

However, as I began to develop my ability to interact with other people, I found this answer incredibly frustrating to deal with. "I don't know" had no substance to build on and would often stop me dead in my tracks when talking to people. In order to address this common sticking point, I had to look back in time to a point when I had to rely on this little phrase.

Why was it, back when I was shy, that I thought "I don't know" was a shiny gem to pull out in any interaction I had with others? Simple. As I said before, it was comfortable and safe and didn't require me to risk saying something "stupid."

More often than not, when I resorted to saying "I don't know," it was out of fear!

SCF X – Tridenting empathizes with this fear your conversation partner may have by explicitly giving them topics. I generally provide three (which is why I call it "tridenting") to give plenty of options, but the number of topics you decide to offer is up to you, as long as it is at least two.

After incorporating this into my day-to-day conversation, I found it is the most useful tool when dealing with indecisiveness. It takes the fear and risk away from your conversational partners and gives them an easy way to respond to you.

Use this SCF and you will be able to hold conversations with chatterboxes and shy guys alike!

Description

Offering multiple responses (usually three) to your conversation partner if they are reluctant to answer.

Benefits

You can get information from someone who is indecisive or having a hard time holding a conversation.

When to Use

When speaking to somebody who remains relatively silent or answers with phrases like "I don't know."

How to Use

After asking a question and receiving no response, provide a few sample answers to draw out a response.

Sample Script

You – What do you want to do today?

Friend – I don't know.

You – Want to go to the park? The movies? To a restaurant?[1]

Friend – I'm not sure.

You – We can do something laid back or outdoors.[2]

Friend – I think I'd like to do something more laid back.

Commentary and Tips

1. In response to "I don't know," you give three options: the park, the movies, and a restaurant.

2. This still did not work, so you gave your friend two broader options—something laid back or something outdoors—to which they replied.

Tip: Repeat this as necessary, as seen in the example above.

Challenge

Easy – Use this with a friend to decide where to eat or what to do.

Medium – Use this with multiple friends to get their decision on where to eat or what to do.

Hard – Use this with a stranger to get their decision on something.

EXIT STRATEGY

SCF 11

◆ ◆ ◆

In addition to learning how to talk to people who are reserved, it is equally as important to learn how to get out of a conversation with people who will talk your ear off.

Don't get me wrong, I love conversations with just about anybody. Unfortunately, sometimes duty calls. A plane won't wait for you, a meeting will start without you, and time doesn't stop and wait to hear what happens next.

However, many of us, myself included, fear being rude or disruptive when we have to leave a conversation prematurely. This consideration for others takes a toll on our time and duties and can be just plain frustrating. I came to understand that if I wanted my time back ...

. . . I had to figure out a way to remove myself from certain conversations in a way that was considerate of other people.

SCF XI – Exit Strategy addresses this concern by preparing ways to exit a conversation without giving offense. In addition, it assertively enforces your need for your time, leaving the risk of inconsiderateness in the court of your conversational partner.

If you need to drop out of a discussion to speak with that guy who can connect you to your dream job, get to a meeting on time, or simply have your day back for yourself, SCF XI – Exit Strategy is going to be a great asset to you.

As important as it is to carry on a conversation, knowing how to end it will preserve your reputation and spare the feelings of those with whom you are speaking.

Description

Strategies for exiting a conversation.

Benefits

You will have a tactful way to exit unproductive or untimely conversation.

When to Use

Whenever you are in a conversation that you need to leave or whenever you must enter a conversation with somebody who likes to talk too much.

How to Use

Two of the easiest and most effective are:

For conversations you are already in:

Cut off + Excuse + Time limit + Tactful goodbye

"Sorry to cut you off, but I'm actually supposed to meet a friend in [number of] minutes and need to get going to get there on time. Would love to pick this up later!"

For conversations you are going to enter with

a known chatterbox:

Time limit + Excuse (optional) + Opener

"Hey, FYI I can only chat for fifteen minutes, but I'd still like to take the time to catch up while we can!" (Then use the defined time frame to exit tactfully).

Sample Script

You – Hey Dave, glad to see you. Unfortunately, I only have five minutes to chat before I have to head down the road to meet up with an old friend. But I'd love to know how you've been!

Dave – (Talks on and on for five minutes)

You – Hey, sorry to cut you off but I have to make my way over to my friend and meet him in two minutes. I can't believe that happened to you! I'd love to pick up on this later![1]

Commentary and Tips

1. A combination of the two frameworks gave notice to Dave that time was limited and allowed

you to break free when time was up. Notice the following.

"I only have five minutes" is the time limit.
"Meeting an old friend" is an optional excuse thrown in afterward.
"But I'd love to know how you've been" is the opener.

"Sorry to cut you off" is the cutoff.
"Make my way over to my friend" is the excuse.
"Two minutes" is the time limit.
"I can't believe that happened to you" is optional detail to show you were listening and not preoccupied with leaving.
"I'd love to pick up on this later" is the tactful goodbye.

Tip: Talking about a point that was covered in the conversation (such as whatever happened to Dave) is a great way to prove to your conversation partner that you were interested in the conversation and your departure is necessary, not meant to get away from them.

Challenge

Easy – Exit a conversation with a friend after a topic has naturally ended.

Medium – Exit a conversation with a stranger after a topic has naturally ended.

Hard – Exit a conversation with a stranger mid–topic.

NOW WHAT?

◆ ◆ ◆

Congratulations on making it through the SCFs! I hope you found them a beneficial resource to aid in you in bettering your conversational skills.

However, I believe that theory by itself will only get you so far. To obtain the full benefits of what this book is presenting, I have included challenges and worksheets to put these principles into practice.

As mentioned in the "How to Use This Book" section, I recommend doing the worksheets in the Appendix before the challenges that were present at the end of each SCF – the worksheets are designed to lower the barrier of entry of talking to people as well as help you establish a strong foundation in conversation.

Take the time to do them and you will pick up on what each SCF is specialized in as well as how they tie together. Excited?

Alixander Laffredo-Dietrich

Let's get to it!

PART III

Appendix

REAL CURIOSITY

Part A:

Listen to an episode from a podcast or interview and list four things you learned about the interviewee. Circle the two that interest you most.

Part B:

Create two questions or statements for each of the things you learned about the interviewee.

I: _____

II: _____

III: _____

IV: _____

INTEREST OPENERS

Part A:

Turn the questions below into Interest Openers.
Note: If done correctly, they will turn into statements

Q I: (Original) How did the meeting go yesterday?

Q I: (Interest) _____

Q II: (Original) Where do you normally go for lunch?

Q II: (Interest) _____

Q III: (Original) Do you like coffee?

Q III: (Agreement) _____

KEEP IT
OPEN

Part A:

Make the questions below open-ended.

Q I: (Original) Do you like ice cream?

Q I: (Open) _____

Q II: (Original) Have you graduated from university?

Q II: (Open) _____

Q III: (Original) Are you from New York City?

Q III: (Open) _____

TOPICS
STORAGE AND
REFERRAL

Part A:

Read the following passage and highlight three topics in yellow:

"I remember that episode! You're talking about the one where they find out it wasn't Arthur's character at all, right? Stellar writing by whoever made that show. I wish I could create stories like that. I wrote down a few ideas back when I was taking creative writing classes to fill out my English credits for my undergrad, but nothing close to that caliber."

Part B:

Write two ways to refer to each topic.

Topic I: _____

Topic I: _____

Topic II: _____

Topic II: _____

TOPICS
NODES

Part A:

Pick any topic to talk about and put it in the pentagon. Extrapolate
five characteristics from this topic and place them in the squares.

Part B:

Extrapolate two additional topics per characteristic you just
created and write them in the circles.

TOPICS
AMPLIFICATION

Part A:

Listen to an episode from a podcast, interview, or discussion on a topic of interest to you.

Part B:

Write three conversational topics that focus on what you have in common with the speaker:

I: _____

II: _____

III: _____

Part C:

Write two nodes for each of these topics that you could speak on.

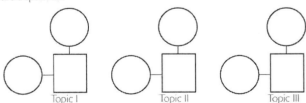

Topic I   Topic II   Topic III

TOPICS
MUTING

Part A:
Read the following passage and highlight topics to mute in yellow:

> "I'm not really into food festivals; I always get sick whenever I go. There was an exception though. I remember there was this awesome festival in North Carolina. Lots of BBQ which, for me, is an automatic win. I plan on going again - it's supposed to be running again two Saturdays from now. I just hope that they don't charge that ridiculous $40 entrance fee. Either way, I suppose it'd be worth it."

Part B:
Circle one topic each to store and refer; node, and amplify.

Part C:
Write one question or statement to transition the talk for each of the topics you circled.

Remember the formula: Empathy Statement + New Topic Transition + New Topic.

I: _____

II: _____

III: _____

TOPICS WEAVING

Part A:

Listen to an interview on television or Youtube and write down the topics the interviewer uses to dig deeper and learn more personal things about their interviewee.

Part B:

Next to each topic you wrote down, label it depending on what level they transitioned to.

Small Talk, Fact Disclosure, Viewpoints and Opinions, and Personal Feelings (Toastmasters International)

Part A:

Turn these questions into Plural Asks.

Q I: (Original) What is your favorite movie?

Q I: (Plural) _____

Q II: (Original) Which country would you like to visit next?

Q II: (Plural) _____

Q III: (Original) What would you like to do today?

Q III: (Plural) _____

TRIDENTING

Part A:

Trident topics to these common questions as if
countering an indecisive response such as "I don't know."

You: What do you want to eat?

Them: *I don't know...*

You: (Trident)

    I.

    II.

Part B:

Trident based off a node from your responses to
simulate if your partner is still unsure.

E.g. If you suggested Mexican food, you could chose restaurants as the node and trident specific names like Chipotle, Qdoba, Chuy's

    I.

    II.

EXIT STRATEGY

Part A:

Create an exit strategy for getting out of a
conversation that has already been started.

Use the formula:
Cut Off + Excuse + Time Limit + Tactful Goodbye

Exit Strategy for Current Conversation:

(Cut off)   (Full Version)

(Excuse)

(Time)

(Goodbye)

Part B:

Create an exit strategy for getting out of a
conversation with a person who is known
to be talkative.

Use the formula:
Time Limit + Excuse (Optional) + Opener

Exit Strategy for Entering Conversation:

(Time)   (Full Version)

(Excuse)

(Opener)

REFERENCES

❖ ❖ ❖

Blatner, Adam. "ABOUT NONVERBAL COMMUNICA-TIONS." Nonverbal Communications, 29 June 2009, www.blatner.com/adam/level2/nverb1.htm.

"Chapter 15 – Evolution of Nonverbal Communication in Hominids." Language Evolution, 22 Mar. 2017, blogs.ntu.edu.sg/hss-language-evolution/wiki/chapter-15/#3_Non-verbal_Communications.

"Conversing with Ease." Toastmasters International.

"Dictionary by Merriam–Webster: America's Most-Trusted Online Dictionary." *Merriam–Webster*, Merriam–Webster, www.merriam-webster.com/.

Jackendoff, Ray. "FAQ: How Did Language Begin?" *Linguistic Society of America*, www.linguisticsociety.org/resource/faq-how-did-language-begin.

Wertheim, Edward G. "The Importance of Effective Communication." Northeastern University, College of Business Administration, 10 Oct. 2008.

ABOUT THE
AUTHOR

◆ ◆ ◆

Alixander Laffredo–Dietrich is more than just a funny name—he is an entrepreneurial artist who bridges the gap between pragmatism and creativity. In other words, he likes using the best of both sides of his noggin to solve any problem in any solution.

As a shy guy turned social enthusiast, his main focus is dissecting soft skills and presenting them in a way that is accessible to all people, from those riddled with social anxiety to the most socially comfortable people.

This is why he created Galhad, an online platform dedicated to teaching soft skills in a structured curriculum. He has taught workshops at colleges on topics ranging from basic communications to job-hunting and does private coaching to help people overcome their biggest obstacles when it comes soft skills.

Alixander has also developed his own skills through various means, from formal organizations such as Toastmasters International to personal trial and error. He shares his reflections and techniques via his Communication Skills 101 series of books as well as speeches he has given at IBM, TEDx, and college universities.

For more information, visit:
www.galhad.com

CERTIFICATE OF COMPLETION

Certificate of Completion

Awarded to

_____

for completion of

"Communications Crash Course"

GALHAD

_____ _____
Start Date   Date Complete

DID YOU ENJOY THIS BOOK?

◆ ◆ ◆

If you found this book helpful and enjoyable, I would appreciate it immensely if you would leave me a quick review on Amazon. The feedback you provide is not only something that I am greatly thankful for, but also helps me know what I should continue doing and what I can improve on. If you would be willing to share your two cents, you can do it **on Amazon!**

www.amazon.com/dp/B07Q4GPPJ9

Thank you so much for taking the time to read this book.

You are the best!

www.galhad.com

Made in the USA
Middletown, DE
30 July 2019